Collins **easy learning**

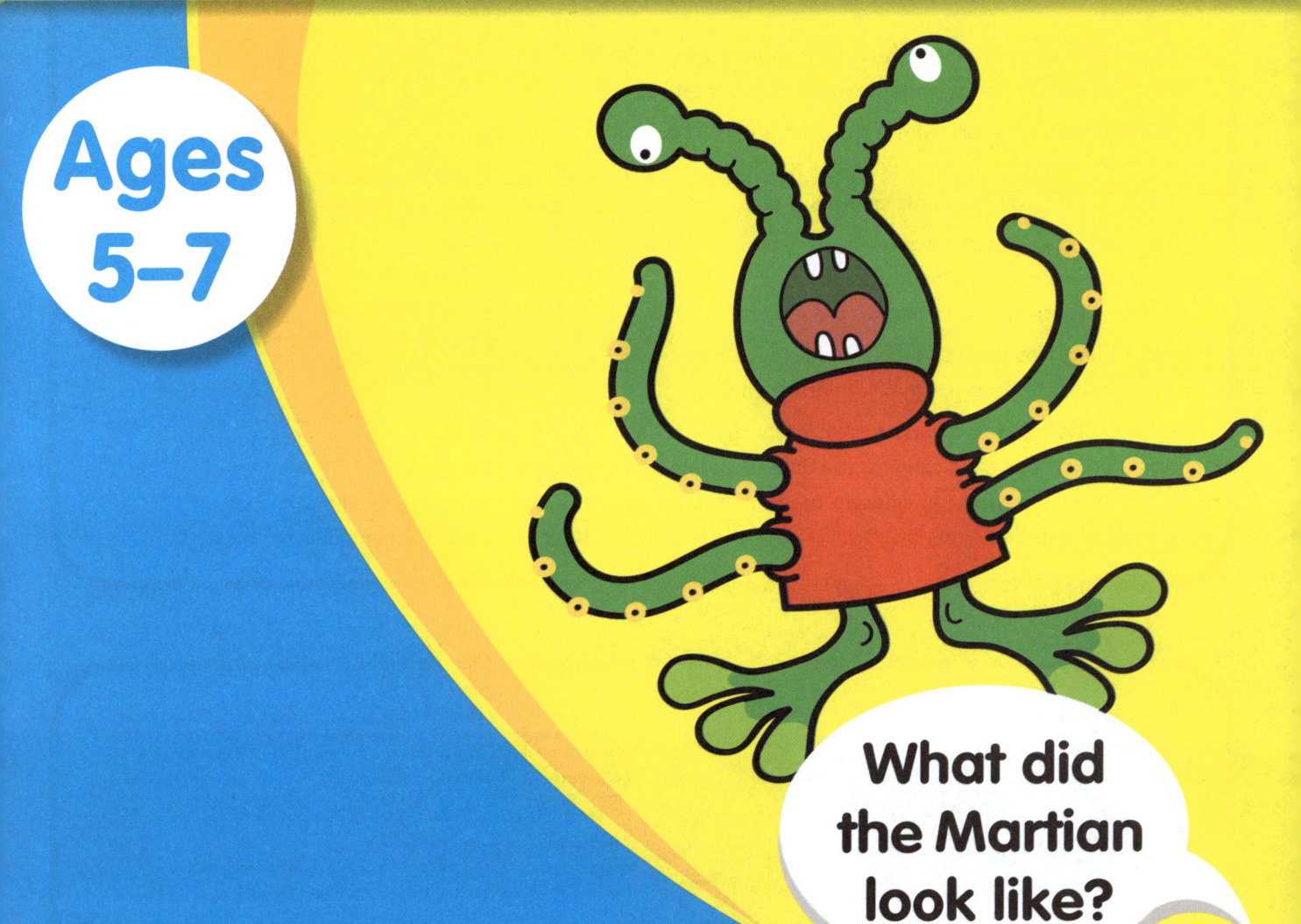

Comprehension

Ages 5–7

What did the Martian look like?

How to use this book

- Find a quiet, comfortable place to work, away from distractions.
- Tackle one extract at a time.
- It is important that your child reads the extract and questions carefully.
- Help with reading the extract and instructions where necessary, and ensure your child understands what to do.
- Encourage your child to check their own answers as they complete each activity.
- Discuss your child's answers with them.
- Let your child return to their favourite pages once they have been completed. Talk about the extracts.
- Reward your child with plenty of praise and encouragement.

Comprehension

Comprehension exercises teach children important skills.

Comprehension questions cover three main categories:

1. *Literal questions* are where the child is required to find and summarise information from the extract.
2. *Inferential questions* are where the child is required to make deductions and predictions from the information provided in the extract.
3. *Evaluative questions* are where the child is required to criticise, empathise with, and relate their own experiences to the extract.

This book includes a mixture of these question types so that your child becomes familiar with each one.

This book also includes a variety of different types of text so that your child can practise understanding and answering questions on different types of text (see table alongside).

Page	Comprehension focus
4	Pictures – fiction
5	Pictures – fiction
6	Pictures – non-fiction
7	Pictures – non-fiction
8	Rhyming poetry
9	Story with a familiar setting
10	Instructions
11	Short playscript
12	Rhyming poetry
13	Recount
14–15	Traditional fairy story
16–17	Dictionary page
18–19	Poem by a significant author
20–21	Fantasy story
22–23	Recount – email
24–25	Playscript of a traditional story
26–27	Explanation
28–29	Story from a different culture
30–31	Poem with familiar settings

Published by Collins
An imprint of HarperCollins*Publishers*
1 London Bridge Street
London SE1 9GF

Browse the complete Collins catalogue at www.collins.co.uk

© HarperCollins*Publishers* 2011
This edition © HarperCollins*Publishers* 2015

10 9 8

ISBN 978-0-00-813430-3

The publisher wishes to thank the following for permission to use copyright material:

David Higham Associates Limited for an extract from *Judy and the Martian* by Penelope Lively, Hodder Wayland, 1992, copyright © 1992 Penelope Lively; *Ice Lolly* by Pie Corbett, copyright © Pie Corbett; The Three Billy Goats Gruff, Looking at a dictionary, Looking after your bike, Hippo and Monkey copyright © John Jackman; p6, 10 and 16 © iStockphoto.com; p16 © Yayayoyo/shutterstock.com

Every effort has been made to trace copyright holders and to obtain their permission for the use of copyright material. The author and publishers will gladly receive any information enabling them to rectify any error or omission in subsequent editions.

All rights reserved. No part of this publication may be reproduced, stored in a retrieval system, or transmitted, in any form or by any means, electronic, mechanical, photocopying, recording or otherwise, without the prior permission of Collins.

British Library Cataloguing in Publication Data

A Catalogue record for this publication is available from the British Library

Page design by G Brasnett, Cambridge and Contentra Technologies
Illustrated by Kathy Baxendale
Cover design by Sarah Duxbury and Paul Oates
Cover illustration by Kathy Baxendale
Project managed by Katie Galloway and Sonia Dawkins
Contributor: Rachel Grant

Printed in Great Britain by Martins the Printers

Contents

How to use this book	2
What next?	4
Family	5
Raining again!	6
What do I do?	7
I eat my peas with honey	8
Going on holiday	9
Sandwich making	10
The new puppy	11
Mary's lamb	12
Oranges	13
The Three Billy Goats Gruff	14
Looking at a dictionary	16
Ice lolly	18
A Martian lands on Earth	20
Wish you were here!	22
Run, run…	24
Looking after your bike	26
Hippo and Monkey	28
What is pink?	30
Answers	32

What next?

1 Look at the pictures. Draw a line to the picture that shows what happens next.

2 Look at the picture. Draw a picture to show what you think happens next.

Family

Look at the pictures.

Tom's family

Dan's family

Meena's family

Jane's family

1 Who lives with their Nan? Circle the answer.

Tom   Meena   Jane   Dan

2 Who has a baby sister? Circle the answer.

Tom   Meena   Jane   Dan

3 Who has two big brothers? Circle the answer.

Tom   Meena   Jane   Dan

4 Who lives with only their Mum and Dad? Circle the answer.

Tom   Meena   Jane   Dan

Raining again!

Jacob made a weather chart.

Monday	🌧️ ☁️
Tuesday	🌧️
Wednesday	☀️
Thursday	☁️
Friday	🌧️ ☁️
Saturday	☀️ 🌧️ ☁️
Sunday	🌧️ ☁️

1 Did it rain on Saturday? Circle the answer.   yes   no

2 Did the sun shine on Tuesday? Circle the answer.   yes   no

3 Did it rain on five days? Circle the answer.   yes   no

4 How many days had white clouds? _____

What do I do?

Circle the answers.

1 I put out fires.
doctor		teacher		**fireman**

2 I sell things.
shopkeeper		teacher		author

3 I teach.
fireman		footballer		**teacher**

4 I write books.
doctor		**author**		shopkeeper

5 I help sick people.
fireman		author		**doctor**

6 I play football.
footballer		shopkeeper		doctor

I eat my peas with honey

I eat my peas with honey;
I've done it all my life.
It makes the peas taste funny,
But it keeps them on the knife.

Anon

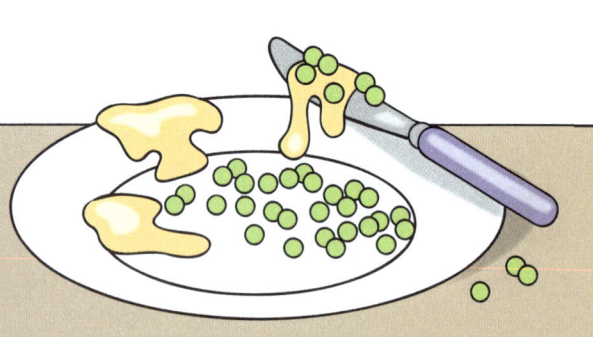

Copy the right answer.

1 The peas are eaten with _____.

carrots   honey   beans

2 The peas taste _____.

funny   yummy   nice

3 The honey keeps the peas on the _____.

plate   fork   knife

Going on holiday

Jess and Alex were happy.
Today they were going on holiday on a boat.

They packed the car and set off.
Dad left a bag behind!

Then they got stuck in traffic.

Oh dear, the boat left without them!
They went home feeling sad.

The next day they got another boat.
Now they were happy.

Copy the right answer.

1 How were Jess and Alex going on holiday? _____.

by boat   **by plane**   **by lorry**

2 Who left the bag behind? _____.

Mum   **Dad**   **Jess**

3 Did the first boat leave without them? _____.

yes   **no**

9

Sandwich making

You will need:
- bread
- butter
- salad
- cheese

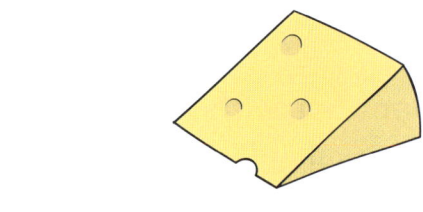

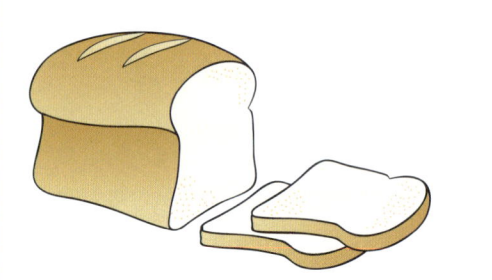

1 Get two slices of bread.
2 Butter each slice of bread on one side.
3 Put the salad and the cheese on one slice.
4 Place the other slice of bread on top.
5 Cut the sandwich in half.
6 Enjoy eating your sandwich!

Copy the right answer.

1 How many slices of bread do you need? _____.

    one   two   three

2 What do you put in the sandwich? _____.

    cheese   salad   salad and cheese

3 When do you eat the sandwich? Tick (✓) the right answer.

When the bread has butter on it. ☐

When the cheese is added. ☐

After the sandwich is cut in half. ☐

The new puppy

Mum Come on Amil, we need to go out.
Amil But Mum, I'm playing.
Mum Sorry, but we have to go.

Amil Where are we going?
Mum You will see!

Amil Why are we here?
Mum You will see!

Mum Are you glad you came with me now?
Amil Yes! I love my new puppy.

Write **yes** or **no** to answer the questions.

1. Did Amil want to go with his mum? _____

2. Did Amil know where he was going? _____

3. Was a man holding the puppy? _____

4. Was Amil pleased with his puppy? _____

Mary's lamb

Mary had a little lamb,
Its fleece was white as snow,
And everywhere that Mary went
The lamb was sure to go;
He followed her to school one day –
That was against the rule,
It made the children laugh and play
To see the lamb at school.

Sarah Josepha Hale

Copy the right answer from the box.

> school   **Mary**   snow

1 Who did the lamb follow? _____

2 What was the lamb's fleece as white as? _____

3 Where did the lamb go? _____

Answer **yes** or **no**.

4 Was the lamb allowed at school? _____

Oranges

Did you know oranges grow on trees?
The trees grow in hot countries.
Flowers grow on the trees.
If it rains and the sun is warm, the flowers grow into oranges.
It takes about eight weeks for a flower to turn into an orange.

Copy the right answer.

1 Where do oranges grow? _____

   on trees   in the ground   on a bush

2 What grows into an orange? _____

   a leaf   a flower   a seed

3 What is needed for oranges to grow? _____

   a hot sun   lots of rain   warm sun and rain

4 Do oranges grow in cold countries? _____

   yes   no

The Three Billy Goats Gruff

The three Billy Goats Gruff had eaten all the leaves. They were getting very hungry.

"Look, there are lots of fresh green leaves across the stream."

"Let's cross the bridge and eat the leaves."

"No! An ugly old troll is under the bridge. If we cross the bridge he will eat us up."

"I am very hungry. I am going to cross the bridge. I'm not afraid of the ugly old troll."

Trip, trap, trip, trap, went Little Billy Goat Gruff.

"Who is that on my bridge?"

"It's me! Little Billy Goat Gruff."

Use a word from the box to finish each sentence.

> troll   hungry   leaves   bridge

1. The three Billy Goats Gruff were _____.

2. They had eaten all the _____ in their field.

3. Little Billy Goat Gruff wanted to cross the _____.

4. A _____ lived under the bridge.

Write **yes** or **no** to answer the questions.

5. Were there two Billy Goats Gruff? _____

6. Is Little Billy Goat Gruff the only hungry one? _____

7. Does Little Billy Goat Gruff try to cross the bridge first? _____

8. Is the troll young? _____

9. How do you think the troll felt when Little Billy Goat Gruff went on the bridge?

_____

_____

_____

_____

Looking at a dictionary

Here are two pages from a dictionary. Read the words and their definitions.

ever	always, for all time
every	all, each one
examination	1) a test
	2) a close look
excellent	very, very good
excuse	a reason for doing or not doing something
expect	to think something will happen
explode	to blow up
eye	the part of the body you see with

Ff	
face	1) the front part of the head
	2) to look towards
fact	something that is true
factory	a building where things are made
fail	not to do something that you try to do
fair	1) blond or light in colour
	2) just, honest
fall	to drop down

abcdefg
hijklm
nopqrst
uvwxyz

Circle the answers.

1 Which is the first word that begins with **f**?

fall   face   fact

2 Which word comes after the word **expect**?

explode   excuse   ever

3 Which word comes before the word **factory**?

fail   fact   fair

4 How many words begin with **fa**?   4   5   6

5 How many words have more than one meaning?   3   4   5

6 Draw a line to link each word to its meaning.

every	to blow up
excellent	blond or light in colour
explode	to look towards
fact	all
face	something that is true
fair	very, very good

Add these words to the dictionary page. Which word would they come after?

7 explore   _____

8 fade   _____

9 faint   _____

Ice lolly

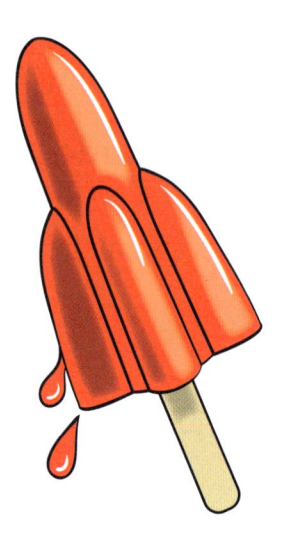

Red rocket
on a stick,
If it shines,
lick it quick.

Round the edges,
on the top,
round the bottom,
do not stop.

Suck the lolly
Lick your lips.
Lick the sides
as it drips

off the stick –
quick, quick,
lick, lick –
Red rocket
on a stick.

Pie Corbett

Use words from the box to finish each sentence.

| **lick it quick** | **ice lolly** | **the edges and bottom** |

1 A red rocket is an _____.

2 If it shines you should _____.

3 The poem says to lick round _____.

Which word from the poem rhymes with these words?

4 **stick** rhymes with _____.

5 **stop** rhymes with _____.

Answer the questions.

6 How many times is the word **lick** used?

_____

7 Why does the poem say, **If it shines, lick it quick**?

_____

8 Name something else you need to lick quickly if the sun shines.

_____

9 Do you think the poet likes ice lollies? How do you know?

_____

_____

10 Can you learn some of this poem by heart?

A Martian lands on Earth

It was the middle of the night when the rocket landed in the supermarket car park. The engine had failed. The hatch opened and the Martian peered out. A Martian, I should tell you, has webbed feet, green skin and eyes on the ends of horns like a snail. This one, who was three hundred and twenty-seven years old, wore a red jersey.

He said, "Bother!" He had only passed his driving test the week before and was already losing his way.

He was also an extremely nervous person, and felt the cold badly. He shivered. A car hooted and he scuttled behind a rubbish bin.

It began to rain. He wrapped himself in a newspaper but the rain soon came through that. And then he saw that a sliding door into the back of the supermarket had been left a little bit open, just enough for him to wriggle through.

Extract from Judy and the Martian by Penelope Lively

Tick (✓) the true sentences. Cross (✗) the false sentences.

1. The rocket landed during the day.

2. The rocket landed in a supermarket car park.

3. The Martian was 127 years old.

4. The Martian was very hot.

5. It started to rain.

What did the Martian look like?

6 Skin – _____

Feet – _____

Eyes – _____

Answer the questions.

7 The Martian wore a red jersey. What is another word for 'jersey'?

_____

8 What does the Martian do that shows he was nervous?

_____

_____

9 Why did the Martian go into the supermarket?

_____

_____

10 What do you think the Martian will do next?

_____

_____

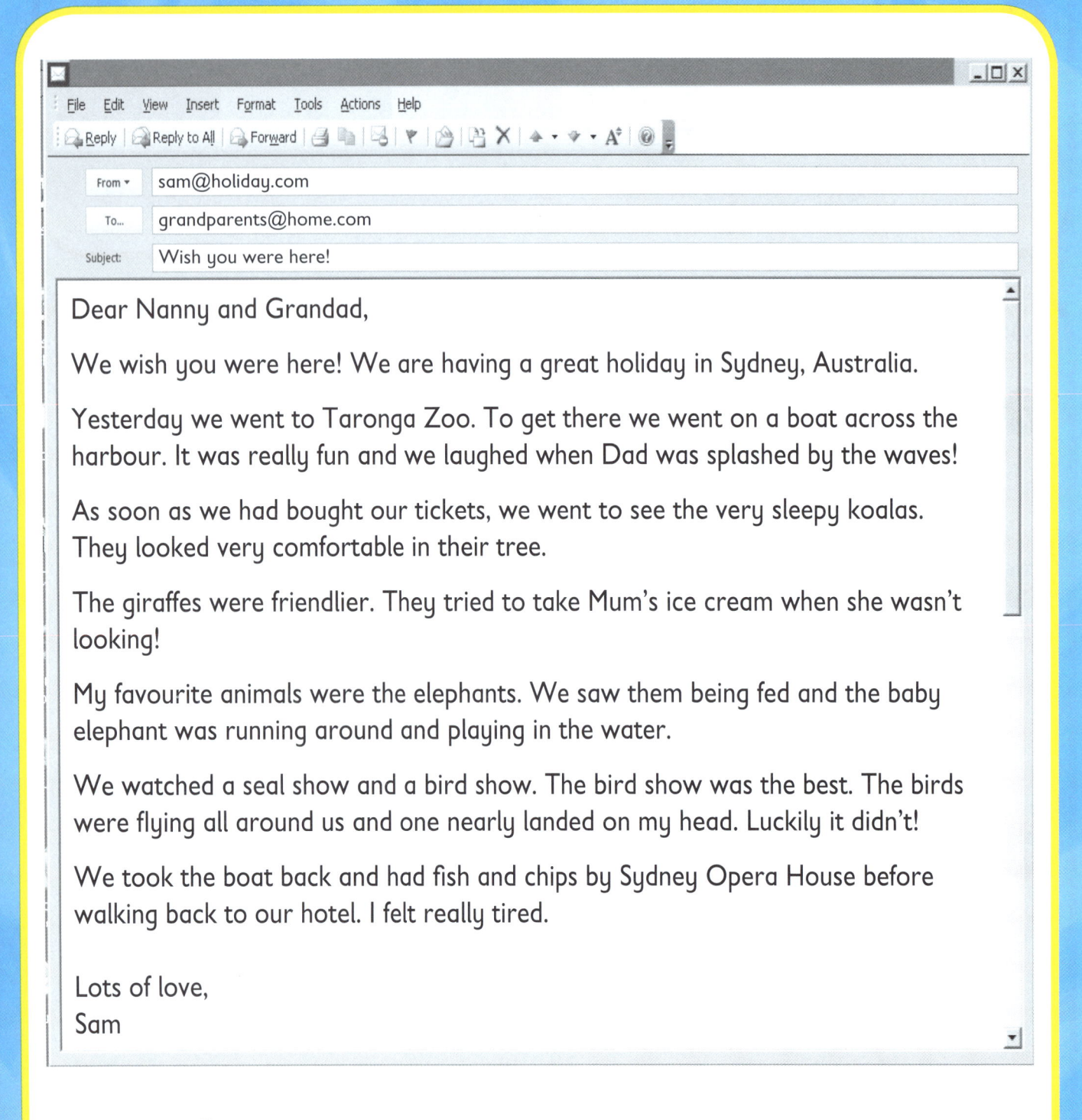

Wish you were here!

From: sam@holiday.com
To: grandparents@home.com
Subject: Wish you were here!

Dear Nanny and Grandad,

We wish you were here! We are having a great holiday in Sydney, Australia.

Yesterday we went to Taronga Zoo. To get there we went on a boat across the harbour. It was really fun and we laughed when Dad was splashed by the waves!

As soon as we had bought our tickets, we went to see the very sleepy koalas. They looked very comfortable in their tree.

The giraffes were friendlier. They tried to take Mum's ice cream when she wasn't looking!

My favourite animals were the elephants. We saw them being fed and the baby elephant was running around and playing in the water.

We watched a seal show and a bird show. The bird show was the best. The birds were flying all around us and one nearly landed on my head. Luckily it didn't!

We took the boat back and had fish and chips by Sydney Opera House before walking back to our hotel. I felt really tired.

Lots of love,
Sam

Tick (✓) the correct answer.

1 Which country is Sam visiting?

Sydney ☐   Taronga ☐   Australia ☐

2 How did Sam get to the zoo?

by car ☐   by boat ☐   by train ☐

3 Which animals were very sleepy?

giraffes ☐   koalas ☐   seals ☐

Answer the questions.

4 Why do you think the elephants were Sam's favourite animals?

_____

_____

5 What did Sam do before going back to the hotel?

_____

_____

6 List **three** things that could have made Sam laugh during the day.

1. _____

2. _____

3. _____

Run, run...

An old lady was cooking a gingerbread man. Suddenly, the gingerbread man jumped out of the oven.

Old lady   Stop! Stop!
Gingerbread man   I'm not going to stop, no one is going to eat me!

The gingerbread man ran out of the back door where Old man was gardening and Cat and Dog were playing.

Old lady   Old man, stop that gingerbread man, it is for your tea.

Old man   I'll try but he's too fast for me! Cat, please stop that gingerbread man.

Cat   I would but I have a claw stuck in a log. Stop, gingerbread man!

Gingerbread man   I'm not going to stop, no one is going to eat me!

Old man   Dog, it is up to you to catch the gingerbread man. Run as fast as you can!

Dog   I'll do my best but I think the gingerbread man is too fast for me.

Gingerbread man   I am fast and I am free. No one is going to eat me for tea!

The gingerbread man came to a river he needed to cross. He saw a fox lying in the sun...

Copy the right answer.

1 Where did the gingerbread man jump? _____

off the table   out of the oven   over the old lady

2 What were Cat and Dog doing in the garden? _____

chasing   playing   gardening

3 Why didn't Cat chase the gingerbread man? _____

her claw was caught   she was too sleepy   she was too slow

4 Number the sentences in the order they happened.

___ The gingerbread man reached a river.

___ The old lady was cooking.

___ Dog could not catch the gingerbread man.

___ The gingerbread man ran out of the back door.

___ Cat's claw was stuck.

5 Why is the gingerbread man running away?

_____

6 What is the weather like?

_____

7 What do you think the fox said to the gingerbread man?

_____

Looking after your bike

A bike is a machine.
All machines need to be looked after carefully.

Tips for looking after your bike

- Clean and dry your bike when it is wet and muddy. This will stop it getting rusty.

- Ask someone to help you to check the brakes. The brakes are very important for your safety.

- Be sure there is enough air in the tyres. When the tyres are soft or flat it is more difficult to keep your balance.

- Make sure the seat is the correct height for you. You should be able to touch the ground with both feet. When you stop you don't want to topple over.

- Always wear your helmet when you ride your bike. If you fall off, your head must be protected.

- Be proud of your bike, and be proud of the way you ride it.

Tick (✓) the true sentences. Cross (✗) the false sentences.

1. If you dry your bike, it will stop it getting rusty. ☐
2. Brakes help you to keep your balance. ☐
3. You should always wear a helmet when you are on your bike. ☐
4. You don't need to look after your bike. ☐

5. Draw a line to link the beginning of the sentences with their correct ending.

Clean your bike   your head if you fall.
A helmet protects   to stay safe on your bike.
Check brakes   it can be hard to balance.
Soft or flat tyres mean to be at the right height.
Your seat needs   to stop it getting rusty.

Answer the questions.

6. What tip do you think is the most important one? Why?

_____

_____

7. List two good things about having a bike.

   1. _____

   2. _____

Hippo and Monkey

Hippo was the strongest of all the animals, so he said he should be Chief. The other animals didn't want Hippo as their Chief. He was too grumpy and moody.

"I bet I can get you out of the pool, Hippo," called Monkey.

"I bet you can't," grunted Hippo. "I'm the strongest animal in the world."
"If I can get you out of the pool, then I should be Chief," said Monkey.
"If you can get me out of the pool, then you can be Chief," said Hippo, "but if I get you into the pool, you will be my servant – forever!"

Off went Monkey to get a really strong rope.
"Hold tight to the rope," said Monkey, "but don't pull until I shout."

Monkey ran into the trees with the other end of the rope.
All the animals watched.
Monkey tied the rope to a big, strong tree trunk.
"Pull!" shouted Monkey. "Pull!"
"This will be easy," thought Hippo to himself.

But all day and all night Hippo pulled, while Monkey sat and ate bananas, and snoozed! Hippo was getting very tired and cross, very cross indeed.
"That monkey must be the strongest monkey I've ever known," thought Hippo.

Slowly he climbed out of the pool, to try to see Monkey.
Just as Hippo took his last foot out of the pool, Monkey ran out of the trees…

1 Write these sentences in the order they happened.

Hippo got out of the pool   Monkey wanted to be Chief.

Hippo got cross.   Hippo pulled on the rope.

Monkey ran out of the trees.   Monkey got a rope.

1. <u>Monkey wanted to be Chief.</u>

2. _____

3. _____

4. _____

5. _____

6. _____

2 Write **T** for the true sentences. Write **F** for the false sentences.

1. Monkey was cleverer than Hippo. _____

2. Monkey won the bet because Hippo was tired. _____

3. Monkey really was the strongest monkey Hippo had ever known. _____

3 What do you think happened next?

_____

_____

What is pink?

What is pink? A rose is pink
By the fountain's brink.

What is red? A poppy's red
In its barley bed.

What is blue? The sky is blue
Where the clouds float through.

What is white? A swan is white
Sailing in the light.

What is yellow? Pears are yellow,
Rich and ripe and mellow.

What is green? The grass is green,
With small flowers between.

What is violet? Clouds are violet
In the summer twilight.

What is orange? Why, an orange,
Just an orange!

Christina Rossetti

Read the poem. Fill in the gap in each sentence.

1 The grass has small _____ between.

2 A white swan sails in the _____.

3 A _____ is yellow and ripe.

4 Yellow rhymes with _____.

5 Between rhymes with _____.

6 Do you like this poem? What do you like or dislike about it?

_____
_____
_____

7 Can you suggest another title for the poem? Explain your answer.

_____
_____

8 Now write your own verse.

Choose a colour. Remember that the last word needs to rhyme with the colour.

What is _____?

_____ is / are _____,

_____.

Answers

What next?
Page 4
1. A line from child making cakes to child eating cake.
   A line from child riding a bike to child having fallen off bike.
   A line from child going to sleep to child waking in morning.
   A line from child looking for lost pet to child finding pet.
2. Child's own picture, e.g. the dog swimming out to get shoe for child.

Family
Page 5
1. Dan
2. Tom
3. Jane
4. Meena

Raining again!
Page 6
1. yes
2. no
3. yes
4. 2 days

What do I do?
Page 7
1. fireman
2. shopkeeper
3. teacher
4. author
5. doctor
6. footballer

I eat my peas with honey
Page 8
1. honey
2. funny
3. knife

Going on holiday
Page 9
1. by boat
2. Dad
3. yes

Sandwich making
Page 10
1. two
2. salad and cheese
3. After the sandwich is cut in half

The new puppy
Page 11
1. no
2. no
3. yes
4. yes

Mary's lamb
Page 12
1. Mary
2. snow
3. school
4. no

Oranges
Page 13
1. on trees
2. a flower
3. warm sun and rain
4. no

The Three Billy Goats Gruff
Page 14–15
1. hungry
2. leaves
3. bridge
4. troll
5. no
6. no
7. yes
8. no
9. Child's own answer, e.g. The troll would feel grumpy after being disturbed.

Looking at a dictionary
Page 16–17
1. face
2. explode
3. fact
4. 6
5. 3
6. every – all
   excellent – very, very good
   explode – to blow up
   fact – something that is true
   face – to look towards
   fair – blond or light in colour
7. explode
8. factory
9. fall